BIBLE VISUALS international

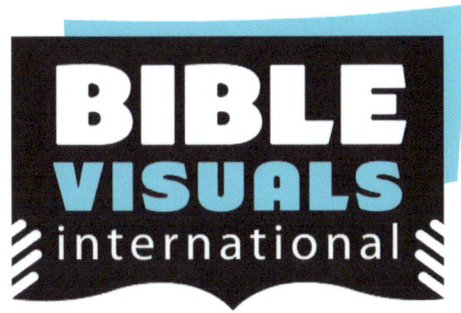

Helping Children See Jesus

ISBN: 978-1-64104-110-2

John and Betty Stam
Missionary Martyrs to China

Author: Karen E. Weitzel
Editors: Audrey Brubaker, Fay Goddard
Illustrators: Vernon Henkel, Linda McInturff
Computer Graphic Artists: Jonathan Ober, Yuko Willoughby
Page Layout: Patricia Pope

© 2020 Bible Visuals International
PO Box 153, Akron, PA 17501-0153
Phone: (717) 859-1131
www.biblevisuals.org

RELATED ITEMS

To access related items (such as activities, memory verse posters and translated texts) please visit our web store at www.biblevisuals.org and enter 5190 at the top right of the web page. You may need to reduce the zoom setting to get the search box.

FREE TEXT DOWNLOAD

To obtain a FREE printable copy of the English teaching text (PDF format) under Product Format, please scroll down and select Extra–PDF Teacher Text Download. Then under Language select English before clicking the ADD TO CART button to place in your shopping cart. Other languages are available at an additional cost from the Language menu. When checking out, use coupon code XTACSV17 at checkout and click on Apply Coupon to receive the discount on the English text.

Great Wall of China

Beijing

Hebei

Yellow Sea

Jinan ○ Qingdao ○

Shandong

Eastern China

Jiangsu

○ Fuyang
○ Yingshan

Yangzhou

Nantong

Anhui

Nanking

Shanghai ○

Wuhu ○

Xuancheng ○

Anqing ○

Jingde ○

Miaosheo ○

Zhejiang

Jiangxi

East China Sea

Chang Jiang River

Fujian

Taiwan

For to me to live is Christ, and to die is gain.

Philippians 1:21

John and Betty Stam
(1907/1906-1934)

This is the story of a young couple who lived for Christ. Betty was six months old when she and her missionary parents left for China. John grew up in Paterson, NJ. After his conversion he helped his father in mission work there. While John and Betty were students at Moody Bible Institute, both felt called to serve as missionaries to China. Betty arrived in China a year before John. After John's first year on the mission field, they were married. Eleven months after that, their daughter was born. Less than three months later, John and Betty were killed by the Chinese Communists. This volume was published in cooperation with the Overseas Missionary Fellowship (formerly known as the China Inland Mission).

The extra activities and review questions to pages 14-16 are correlated with each chapter and encourage student involvement. You may wish to make a copy of the memory verse token on page 10 for each student.

PRONUNCIATION GUIDE

We have chosen to use the old Chinese spelling for these locations as that is what was used in China when John and Betty were there. The new Chinese spelling has been given for some words to help you locate them on a larger, up-to-date map of China.

Old Spelling (New Spelling)	Pronunciation	Old Spelling (New Spelling)	Pronunciation
Anhwei Province (Anhui)	Ann´ - whey	Swenchiapu	Swun´ - ja - poo
Anking (Anqing)	Ann - king´	Tsinan (Jinan)	Je´ - nan
Fowyang (Fuyang)	Fo´ - yahng	Tsingtao (Qingdao)	Ching - dow´
Miaosheo	Mee - ow´ - show	Tsingteh (Jingde)	Ching´ - deh
Pao	Bough	Tungchow (Tungzhou)	Tongue - jo´
Peking (Beijing)	Pea - king´	Wuhu	Woo - hoo´
Shanghai	Shang - high´	Yamen	Yah´ - men
Shantung Province (Shandong)	Shan - dung´	Yangchow (Yangzhou)	Yahng´ - jo
Sinkiang (Xinjiang)	Shin - jiang´	Yangtze River (Chang Jiang River)	Yang´ - see
Suancheng(Zuancheng)	Schwen´ - chung	Yingshang	Ying - shang´

Waves surged ahead of the ship and rolled over each other in a race to reach shore. The dark strip of land hugging the horizon stretched as far as the eye could see. A young couple stood on deck and watched as the rising sun shone on the buildings along the shoreline. "China is a big country, isn't it, Charles?" the woman said softly.

Show Illustration #1

Dr. Scott looked down at his wife and smiled. Gently he shifted the sleeping infant in his arms to protect her from the winds. "Yes, Clara," he answered. "And this is only part of the coast. China extends thousands of miles inland. But we, no doubt, will settle somewhere here on the coast where the Presbyterians have an established work."

The baby cried and Mrs. Scott tucked the blanket around their daughter. "I wonder what it will be like living in China," she said. "For little Betty it won't seem strange. She'll grow up hearing and seeing what now will be new to us. Charles," she said, then paused, "do you suppose China could have another uprising like the Boxer Rebellion? So many missionaries and children were killed then."

Dr. Scott looked out over the choppy sea toward the land to which God had called them. "It's possible," he replied seriously. "That happened only six years ago in 1900. Conditions still are unsettled in China, though there is a different feeling throughout the country. Now, instead of hating foreigners, Chinese are eager to learn. Many are flocking to Christian schools. Missionaries are accepted again, but that could change overnight. Whatever happens, Clara, God will take care of us."

The ship slowly approached the busy harbor where other steamers were docked. Smaller boats crisscrossed the water carrying passengers and goods from ships to the city's wharves. Flat-bottomed junks with dirty ribbed sails and narrow, low-slung houseboats crowded the inner harbor.

The city was also congested. Excited, dark-eyed Chinese gestured and reached for passengers' luggage. Rickshaws pulled by fleet-footed men darted among the carts and pedestrians. The confusing babble of voices surrounded the American couple who planned to make this foreign country their home.

Dr. and Mrs. Scott settled in Tsingtao, a coastal city many miles north of the seaport of Shanghai. After learning the language, Dr. Scott traveled through the surrounding area as an evangelist and Bible teacher. During those years Betty became big sister to Helen, Bunny (Beatrice), Francis and finally Kenneth.

Show Illustration #2

One morning long after breakfast and family prayers, Betty and Helen returned from exploring the nearby woods. Spying their father's old bicycle, they took turns riding it. Helen finally gave up. With both hands, she pushed her brown bobbed hair away from her sticky face.

"My legs aren't long enough to sit on the seat and reach the pedals," she complained.

Betty propped the bicycle beside the house. "In a couple of years you'll be able to ride as well as I can," she said consolingly. She straightened her dress, then patted her short, dark hair in place. Being ten, nearly eleven years old, made her feel almost grown up.

Helen sighed and sat down with a plop on the porch steps. "I'm tired and hungry. Let's go over to the servants' cottage for some Chinese food." She looked expectantly at Betty, her eyes shining, pleading, anticipating the seldom-eaten food.

"Oh, Helen, we shouldn't," Betty said quietly. "It's too close to dinner. And Mother doesn't think that Chinese food is good for us."

"But it tastes good," Helen protested. "You know it does. We wouldn't have to eat a lot. Just a little."

Betty laughed uneasily. "All right. Let's go." After glancing over her shoulder to make sure Bunny or Francis weren't following, she slipped silently around the house with Helen following her. She hoped Mother wasn't watching. As the oldest, she knew Mother expected her to do what was right. But sometimes it was easier to forget that.

Dr. and Mrs. Scott were missionaries to the Chinese, but they also taught their children to know God. Betty, an alert girl, listened eagerly to Bible stories of God's love. She heard her parents pray for the Chinese to understand God's message of salvation. She understood that she had disobeyed God, but now that Jesus was her Saviour, she wanted to obey God.

Show Illustration #3

"You see, Helen and Bunny," Betty began patiently on a warm Sunday afternoon as they sat on the porch steps. "Mother and Father came to China with an important message for the Chinese people. The message is in the Bible. God wants Chinese–and everybody else–in Heaven, but there's only one way for them to get there. Father tells the people that way is believing in Jesus."

"What does that mean?" five-year-old Bunny interrupted, wrapping her doll in a blanket.

"It means," Betty began, "that we believe God loves us and wants us in Heaven. Heaven is a beautiful place, but nobody who does wrong can go there."

Helen looked slyly at Betty. "I guess you won't go there."

"But I shall," Betty said happily. "I know I've done wrong. The Bible says everyone has. But Jesus was punished for all my sin when He died on the cross. Then He was buried and three days later rose again. God says in the Bible if I believe that and ask Him to forgive the wrongs I do, He will. I've done that so now I will go to Heaven."

"Right now?" Bunny asked as if Betty would disappear suddenly. Bunny got up and stood close to Betty.

"No," said Betty, hugging her little sister. "Not right now."

"Good!" Bunny said. "Then can we play with my doll?"

"Yes," Betty said as she walked with Bunny along the path from the house. *It would be easier to ignore her,* Betty thought. *But playing with her instead of doing what I want will please God.*

An older cousin from the United States lived with the Scott family and taught the children. Until Betty was 11 she studied at home. After summer vacation that year she traveled northwest to Tungchow, near Peking (Beijing), and entered the North China American School. Betty adjusted quickly to the new routines and classes at boarding school.

Several years later when Helen joined her, Betty had many friends.

Show Illustration #4

Both girls studied Chinese characters at school. "We might need to know Chinese later, Helen," Betty said thoughtfully as they walked around the campus after classes. "It would help to learn it now just in case God wants us to be missionaries here someday."

"That won't be for a long time, Betty," Helen exclaimed. "You're only 16! With Mother and Father planning furlough next year, and your attending college in the States, it will be years before you can return to China."

"But I can come back knowing a little Chinese." Betty stood still and looked around her. "Leaving China next year makes me sad at times. With so many wars in the country, soldiers, changing governments and the anti-foreign feeling, maybe I'll never return. Then I think of the trip Father is planning and I can't wait to go. Can you imagine traveling for six months around the world? I'm sure we'll see the Tombs of the Kings in Egypt and the Garden Tomb in Palestine where Christ was buried."

"And museums in Italy," Helen interrupted. "Mountain climbing in Switzerland and much more in France and England."

When the six-month trip ended the following August in Springfield, MA, Betty entered her senior year of high school. In the spring she became ill with inflammatory rheumatism and her heart was weakened.

During four months of rest she discovered she could write poetry. As summer began and the days grew hot, she often thought of her family, now back in China and probably at their seaside vacation home. Picking up a pencil, she wrote: "It is hot; along the highroad lies the dust on field and tree, and my heart returns with longing to a cottage by the sea."

There would be no more family outings. Betty was on her own, but not alone for she knew God was with her. In September, though still weak, she arrived at Wilson College, an all-girls' school in Chambersburg, PA. Schedules, classes, and assignments soon tired her so much that she was admitted to the infirmary.

Lying between cool white sheets, Betty was surprised one day to see a student enter her room. The tall girl with light brown, wavy hair smiled as she crossed the room. *She must be an upperclassman,* Betty thought in awe.

"I'm Marguerite," the girl said in a soft, low voice. "I heard you were here and thought you would enjoy a visit with another freshman."

Show Illustration #5

Visits between the girls continued when Betty returned to her dorm room. She spent many hours studying in Marguerite's room that first year. In the fall of her second year, Betty roomed with Marguerite and another student. No more carting books back and forth between rooms!

One evening when the two friends were alone in their room, Betty closed the books on her desk and looked across the room. Marguerite was staring intently at a textbook, her elbows holding the book open and her chin resting on her hand.

"It must be biology," Betty said with a laugh. "You'll be a nurse yet."

Marguerite sighed and closed the book. "That's it for tonight, though." She glanced at Betty. "Is something on your mind?"

Betty smiled as she adjusted her round, dark-rimmed glasses. "I thought I'd tell you what happened at America's Keswick this summer."

"We haven't had much time to talk since classes began," Marguerite remarked.

"I had a great time meeting other young people at the youth conference," Betty began. "And we had such fun canoeing on the pond and walking beneath the pines. But what impressed me most were the messages I heard and the prayer times morning and evening. God used one verse in Philippians to change me inside out." Betty pulled her Bible toward her and read softly, "To me to live is Christ, and to die is gain."

"I've noticed you were different," Marguerite said.

"You have?" Betty asked eagerly. "I hoped it would show. I mean, I want others to see the difference in my life. Before this summer, I often thought about having a good time. I wanted lots of attention and compliments. But at America's Keswick (a Bible conference center in Whiting, New Jersey) I understood that God wants me to live, not for Betty, but for Him. I now let the Lord take charge of my life. Every morning I read my Bible to find out what God wants me to do. I don't know what He has in store for me, but I've begun praying that if God wants me in China as a missionary, nothing will keep me from going."

With that as her goal, Betty became involved in the Student Volunteer Movement at college. Along with Marguerite and other girls who planned to go to the mission field, Betty took her turn leading devotions during their meetings.

Betty was quiet, yet popular, among the girls. Her radiant smile and interest in others made students want to tell her their problems. Often they returned to their rooms thinking about a Bible verse Betty had shared with them.

The summer before her senior year, Betty returned to New Jersey. At a YWCA camp she became one of the counselors for junior and senior high girls. The bugler for the camp was a rough and tumble girl for whom Betty prayed. Before camp was over, she had won Billie's confidence and led her to the Lord.

Leading people to Christ was what Betty wanted to do most of all. So, upon graduating from Wilson College in 1928, she enrolled at Moody Bible Institute in Chicago. After classes, Betty joined other students and visited prisons or participated in street meetings. There she talked to people about how they could know the Lord Jesus Christ.

Show Illustration #6

Monday evenings Betty joined other young people interested in China. Together they rode the train to the home of Dr. and Mrs. Isaac Page. As missionaries and District Secretary of the China Inland Mission, the Pages held a prayer group for any wanting to pray for mission work in China. Betty knew that God was calling her to be a missionary in China. She also had noticed a student in the prayer group who appeared to be interested in her. His name was John Stam.

He was praying about going to China as a missionary. And he reminded Betty of a poem she had written about the man she hoped to marry.

"I'll recognize my true love
When first his face I see;
For he will strong, and healthy,
And broad of shoulders be . . .
. . . He will not be a rich man,
He has no earthly hoard;
His money, time, heart, mind and soul
Are given to the Lord . . . ."

I wonder if John might be the man God has chosen for me, Betty thought as they traveled back and forth to the Pages' home each week.

Chapter 2
John Learns to Trust

Show Illustration #7

John stood the shovel in the mound of snow he had just cleared from the walk. His long arms ached and his hands itched from the warm, wool mittens. Scooping a handful of fluffy snow, he patted it into a lopsided ball, then glanced down the hill to see if Father was coming with their guest. A cold wind whistled along the empty street that winter day in 1921. Heavy, gray clouds in the darkening sky looked threatening. "It's going to snow again," John said wistfully.

A yellow glow from the front room windows shone down through the railing of the high porch. John looked up. Amelia's face was pressed against the center window. He tossed the snowball onto the porch, then laughed as his little sister ducked. *Even though I'm 14 and nearly as tall as Father, I still like throwing snowballs,* he thought. Grabbing the shovel, he stomped the snow from his feet, then ran up the porch steps two at a time.

The houses on Temple Hill looked out over the city of Paterson, New Jersey. The Stam home was the highest on the hill. In warmer weather John and his younger brother Neal sometimes climbed to the cupola over the attic to see the New York skyline in the distance. But in winter it was warmer in the living room.

Show Illustration #8

John removed his coat. By the time he had placed Bibles on the dinner table beside each plate, Father had arrived with their guest. John slid into his seat. A short, heavyset man sat down beside his tall father. Father turned towards him. "Brother, we are accustomed to reading the Scriptures before meals. Will you begin the readings this evening? Each of us will read three verses from our Bible. That is," he paused, "unless someone makes a mistake. When that happens, the person loses his turn."

The man chuckled. "Gladly, Mr. Stam, gladly will I read. And I shall try not to let the words trip on my tongue. I am not used to speaking so much English, just having returned to America from the mission field."

The meal was lively for the missionary had much to tell about his experiences overseas.

After dinner and prayer, the family remained at the table listening to their guest. "I did not know," he continued, "that when I trusted in Jesus as my Saviour, God would send me to Africa one day. But I am glad He did. It is a joy to tell men and women about the Lord Jesus. You must have that same joy, Brother Stam, in your work at the Star of Hope Mission. But you have not always been in mission work."

Father cleared his throat. "No. After I arrived in America from Holland as a young man, I took a job as a carpenter. The work expanded into the lumber business now behind our home. At first, in my spare time I gave Christian literature to Jews in Paterson. As men and women from area churches joined my efforts, we sought to witness to others. Eventually it became necessary to purchase a building in the center of Paterson. That is where all our Bible meetings are held." He looked around the table. "Most of our eight children help in the ministry. Peter, the one over there, and Clazina, Henry, Jacob, and even Harry participate in the open-air meetings and visitation."

The missionary looked across the table at John. "And you will follow, too, witnessing like your older brothers and sister?" he asked the dark-haired lanky youth.

John squirmed in his seat. "Y-yes, I s-suppose so, sir," he replied.

Show Illustration #9

Sundays the family attended the Christian Reformed Church. After church, they enjoyed quiet activities.

That Sunday afternoon John looked longingly at the snow outside. Sledding was not a Sunday activity. He pulled a book from the bookcase and sprawled on the living room rug. Neal and Amelia were looking at pictures in the stereoscope.

"Here's a picture of Africa," Neal exclaimed, holding the viewer for Amelia to see.

"Let's have a look," John said, reaching for the handle.

"Would you want to be a missionary, John?" Neal asked. "It sounds exciting, but I think it would be hard."

"I don't know," John replied. "I guess it's hard work. That's what the missionary said last night."

Neal nodded as he spoke. "He said something about trusting God to supply his needs. What did he mean?"

John sat up and handed the viewer to Neal. "I'm not real sure." He hesitated. His brothers or Clazina could answer that question, but they weren't around. "Maybe he meant . . . . Remember the story about when Father told his boss he would not work on Sunday? Father got fired, but he knew God would provide the money for food and clothes and things though he didn't know how. And that night another boss Father had worked for earlier hired him for more money. Father did what he knew was right and believed God would provide another job."

"Could you trust God like that, John?" Neal asked.

"I don't know. Maybe some day I'll have to," he replied. "But now I'm learning so much at Drake Business School that I'm sure I'll always have a job."

John graduated from the Christian Grammar School in Paterson when he was 13. He chose to study business for two years. Hopes of working at a job and earning money filled his mind and motivated him to study.

But he was not as diligent in attending meetings at his father's mission. Excuse after excuse kept him out of the large hall where drunkards and other people were being converted. He was not a drunkard! He had always gone willingly to church and catechism classes. He knew about God. That was enough for him.

Show Illustration #10

I won't help in or even go near the open-air meetings, John vowed as he walked home from school one afternoon. *It's all right for Henry and Harry and the others, but not for me.* As he turned the corner of the block, the swelling music from a pump organ made him stop suddenly and duck into a doorway. He leaned forward cautiously and peered around the corner.

A group of mission workers were distributing tracts to pedestrians at the end of the block. Clazina sat at the portable organ. Henry had walked into the street to a car that had stopped beside the crowd. John saw his brother hand the passengers a tract, then jump aside as the highly polished, black sedan started forward. The car rumbled past John. One of the ladies thrust her hand out the open window and dropped the crumpled tract. It bounced off the running board into the gutter. "Ridiculous!" John heard her exclaim indignantly. " 'Repent,' it said. I am not going to repent before God."

John stared soberly at the gutter. He had thought those words, too. A gust of wind blew the wrinkled tract down the street. John couldn't help but remember a verse from that morning's Bible reading. *The Lord is not willing that any should perish, but that all should come to repentance.* The way his father had read those words, then looked at John, had made him uncomfortable. Turning quickly, he darted around the corner and walked blocks out of his way to avoid the street meeting.

John continued to ignore God until the end of May. But that last Sunday he ran out of excuses for skipping meetings. Besides, the blind evangelist who was to speak at the mission hall that evening aroused John's curiosity. At dinner that day John had watched the Rev. Thomas Houston eat his meal as normally as if he could see.

That night the tall youth, now 15, walked with his family to the mission. John sat in the last row, and as Rev. Houston spoke, he felt farther from God than ever. *It's because of my sin that I feel so far from God,* he realized. *I've been ignoring God and trying to live without Him. I've never really trusted Him. And if I do not turn to Him now for forgiveness, I shall one day be separated forever from Him.* The awfulness of hell made him understand why Jesus died to be his Saviour.

No one around him knew that night that John had confessed his sin and decided to follow God. But soon they learned of his decision when, self-consciously, he began participating in mission work.

Show Illustration #11

Following graduation from business school, John worked as a stenographer and clerk, first in Paterson, and later in New York City. He became one of the thousands of men and women who rode the trains and ferries to the city. Most commuters on the trains read newspapers or worked crossword puzzles, a new fad that was popular. John read books or studied Greek with several other fellows. Sometimes he looked at the changing New York skyline. Skyscrapers 40 and 50 stories high were competing to be the tallest building.

There was even talk of a monstrous building over 100 stories, but this Empire State Building wouldn't be finished for several years. John watched this progress and became increasingly discontented.

I don't think I should be so caught up in trying to get ahead and make money, he thought as the train rocked and clacked over the tracks. *It's more important to help people find God. Perhaps I should return to school to study the Bible and learn how to preach or teach.*

After working in offices for six years, John resigned from his job in the spring of 1929. He helped his father at the mission that summer, planning to attend Moody Bible Institute in the fall. He had saved enough money to pay for his first year or two at school. When that was gone, he would trust God to provide another job or send what he needed. He would tell no one, not even his family, when his money ran out. At the end of summer he took the train west.

John determined to do well in his studies at Moody and he did. He also learned lessons that didn't come from textbooks. Through chapel messages and student mission prayer groups during his years at school, John learned there were millions of people around the world who did not know the Gospel message.

There were thousands upon thousands in inland China who had never heard of the Lord Jesus Christ. The China Inland Mission was asking for 200 new missionaries to go to China between 1929 and 1931. The Forward Movement, as it was called, appealed to John, and he began attending the weekly CIM prayer meetings on Monday evenings.

Show Illustration #6

"China is a difficult mission field," Dr. Page began one evening. "The country is being torn apart by changing governments. Bandits loot villages and kill people at random. Just two years ago, another anti-Christian movement forced missionaries to flee to the coasts. This feeling has died down now and missionaries are back on their stations. They've discovered that many Chinese Christians remained faithful during the uprising. While the missionaries were gone, the Chinese assumed leadership in the churches."

"But if the Chinese can now lead," a new student interrupted, "are missionaries still needed?"

Dr. Page smiled. "They are needed now more than ever," he replied. "Missionaries will continue to work alongside the Chinese Christians, teaching and giving help when needed. But there are other Chinese ready to listen to the Gospel in cities and villages where there are no Christians or missionaries. We need men to go to the mountain tribes in the west and others to work among the Muslims in Sinkiang. Hudson Taylor, the founder of our mission, said we must be 'always advancing.' Even though mission work in China will not be easy, we must not stop praying for men and women to go to these unreached people."

John bowed his head. *Lord,* he thought, *the need is so great in China. I have no valid reason for staying in the States where there are so many already preaching Your Word. Do You want me in China? Father has wanted me to take charge of the mission back home, but now he is willing to let me go to China if that is where You want me to go.*

After the prayer time ended, Mrs. Page invited the students to stay for refreshments. When her husband began reading aloud from one of his favorite books, John settled back into his chair.

Across the room, Betty Scott was listening intently to Dr. Page. There was something about her that John liked. *Maybe it's her smile*, he thought as he watched her. *She's quiet and gentle and seems interested in me. I'd like to get to know her. But how?* he questioned. *After waiting on tables in the school dining room, typing papers for students and studying, there's little time left. Then, too, Betty is planning to go to China. I'm not sure God is calling me there. It wouldn't be fair to show I'm interested in her if I'm to return to Paterson.*

Later as the students walked through the chilly night on their way back to Moody, John's silence was noticed. "Thinking about China, John?" one of them asked.

"Yes, I am–and no, I'm not," John said hesitantly.

"What kind of answer is that?" the same fellow demanded, laughing with the others as they stood under the streetlight at a corner.

Betty smiled at John. "He could be thinking about China and something else at the same time," she said defending him.

John looked over at Betty and returned her smile. "You're right," he said simply. But he didn't share the "something else."

Returning to his dorm room, John sat at his desk and held his head in his hands. *Lord,* he prayed, *You have been faithful in keeping me out of debt here at Moody. Especially when many in America have struggled to pay bills during this Depression. While so many are unemployed, you have always given me work or sent money through friends–sometimes at the last minute, but never late. Thank You for the money Roy gave for my school bill. And thank You, too, for the five dollar bill I found while crossing Michigan Avenue last Saturday. It was just enough to buy shirts and socks to take home for this Christmas vacation. But Father, I have another request now. It's about Betty. Help me to trust You to make it possible for us to get to know each other.*

Show Illustration #12

Knock, knock, knock.

Betty looked up from her desk as the door opened. A short, smiling, round-faced girl stuck her head around the door.

"Have your paper written yet, Betty?" she asked almost shyly.

"Just about, Faith. Come in. You can have my chair." Betty left her cluttered desk and sat on the bed, tucking one leg under her.

"It looks like you've been busy," Faith commented glancing at the desk.

Betty laughed. "Yes, and I probably would have been finished by now, but I kept thinking about what I said this morning."

"About not having anything decent to wear?" Faith asked gently.

"Yes," replied Betty. She tucked a strand of dark hair into the bun at the back of her neck, then smoothed a wrinkle from her well-worn skirt. "The Lord reminded me of some verses in Matthew and I realized I was complaining about how God cares for my needs."

"Which verses, Betty?" Faith asked quietly.

Betty got up and walked to her desk. Picking up her Bible, she turned several pages then read, " 'And why take ye thought for raiment? Consider the lilies of the field, how they grow; they toil not, neither do they spin: and yet I say unto you, That even Solomon in all his glory was not arrayed like one of these' " (Matthew 6:28-29). She looked at Faith. "I'm sorry for complaining to you. If God can take care of the flowers in the field, then He will surely care for me."

"He surely will," Faith echoed, then added, "both here and in China."

Their conversation was interrupted by the clatter and vibration of the elevated train speeding through their neighborhood. When all was quiet, except for the muffled rumble of cars in the street below, Faith spoke again. "I thought I'd go for a walk this afternoon. Can you join me?"

"Well," Betty said slowly, then blushed.

"You have other plans?" Faith asked as she stood.

"Yes," Betty replied. "Oh, Faith, I'd love to walk with you. But I've told John I'm free this afternoon. We'll probably walk down along Lake Michigan."

"That's fine!" Faith exclaimed agreeably as she opened the door. Turning, she added, "You really like him, don't you? You've been seeing him more often."

Betty smiled as she left.

Show Illustration #13

A cool breeze rippled the lake water near the shore. Farther out, white-capped waves sparkled in the late afternoon sun. Betty and John walked slowly along the edge of the lake.

"How were the services at Elida (Ohio) last weekend, John?" Betty asked when they stopped to look out over the lake.

"The church people seem to enjoy quoting Scripture from memory," John began. "We've been doing that just before the sermon Sundays I'm at the church. Only my heavenly Father knows how this Scripture or my sermons affect the people. While out walking through the town Sunday afternoon, I was able to witness to several people who knew little of God or the Bible."

"Just think, John, how this is preparing you for ministry in China," Betty exclaimed.

"Yes," John replied, "*if* that is where God wants me, and *if* I am accepted by the China Inland Mission." He looked down at Betty a long time. "After graduation next month you leave for CIM candidate school in Philadelphia. You'll probably be accepted and head for China as one of the Forward Movement long before I graduate. As much as I love you, Betty, I don't believe we should marry now. If we married and the mission decides I'm not qualified to be a missionary, it would keep you from going. If the mission does accept me, they will most likely send me, a single man, to where it's too dangerous for women to serve. I can't ask you to be my wife now when my future is still uncertain."

Betty smiled bravely at John. "I understand," she said softly. "We must put God first. We must obey Him. If He wants us to be married, He will bring us together–in China."

It was hard for Betty and John to part after graduation in April 1931. Betty was often in John's thoughts. One night in late May after leading a cottage Gospel meeting on the south side of Chicago, John jotted his thoughts in his diary. *Betty is in Philadelphia, but I have not been able to write her a letter. While Betty and I look forward to serving on the same field, I cannot move one step in her direction until I am sure that it is the Lord's will.*

It was God's will for the couple to see each other before Betty left for China. In mid-October, on her way to the West Coast, Betty stopped in Chicago to see John. They walked along the lake, talked and prayed. As always, John was gentle and considerate. Betty couldn't help loving him even more.

Show Illustration #6

That night they attended the China prayer group at Dr. and Mrs. Page's home. Afterwards, John told the older couple how God had brought them together. "But," he said, "we believe God wants us to go to China separately."

And so, while each loved the other, Betty left John at Moody Bible Institute. She boarded a ship for China when she arrived on the West Coast.

The CIM opened new mission stations when members of the Forward Movement arrived in China. Many soldiers, opium addicts and others were turning to Christ. Chiang Kai-shek, commander of the southern armies, was converted and baptized in the Methodist Church.

The Communists were just as busy spreading propaganda–ideas that opposed the government and the way the Chinese had lived for centuries. Their armies looted homes and villages and fought both the bandits and the army led by General Chiang Kai-shek. Bandits, too, all over China, continued to capture people, rob them, and many times murder them. Being a missionary in China in the early 1930s was difficult and dangerous. Those who were there knew they were risking their lives to tell the Chinese about the Lord.

Show Illustration #14

Winter in Chicago that year was windy and bitterly cold. In Yangchow, China, it was cold too. There in the language school, Betty and 60 other young women, dressed in quilted Chinese gowns, sat near kerosene stoves as they studied. Because Betty had studied Mandarin in high school, she was put in an advanced class with several others who had grown up in China. All the women struggled to imitate the tones and words their Chinese men teachers used. Learning to write the characters was just as difficult.

John faced other difficulties. He found that trusting God for money had to be done over and over. And when John graduated from Moody that spring, he wore not a new suit (that would be too extravagant and expensive) but a mended one.

The tailor was paid with money John received as a gift. But no one noticed the suit as John gave the class address at graduation.

"The Great Commission," he said, "never called for advance only if funds were plentiful and if no hardships or self-denial were involved. We are told to expect tribulation and even persecution. God Himself is with us as our Captain . . . to encourage and to fight for us."

After graduation in 1932, John spent six weeks at the China Inland Mission Home in Philadelphia. In July he was accepted into the mission. Two months later John boarded the *Empress of Japan,* a passenger liner crossing the Pacific Ocean from the West Coast. He and several other new missionaries were finally on their way to China.

During the two and a half weeks it took to cross the ocean, John witnessed to several young men. And when alone, he often thought of Betty. He had not received a letter from her before he left. Did she still feel the same about him? Perhaps there would be a letter for him when he arrived.

In mid-October, the *Empress of Japan* entered Shanghai harbor. John and the other young men were escorted through the crowds to the mission headquarters in the city. The large administration building was impressive. John glanced around the area and thought, *How peaceful after the rush of the people in the streets.* Activity around the Home's entrance caught his attention. A movement so familiar that he would have recognized it anywhere stopped him short.

Show Illustration #15

"Betty," he gasped as she walked toward him. "How is it that you are in Shanghai? I thought, I hoped there might be a letter from you, but this, this is better–a thousand times better."

"Oh, John," Betty said softly, "it's good to see you. The doctor sent me here to have my tonsils removed. That's been taken care of. I'll return in about a week with Mr. and Mrs. Glittenberg to their station at Fowyang."

"Say, John," one of the young men called after observing John's joy in seeing Betty, "how did you work this meeting?"

John laughed. "I–we didn't. This is unexpected, unplanned on our part, but wonderful to be sure. Our heavenly father arranged it for Betty to be here when our ship arrived."

That day John asked Betty to become his wife. The China Director of the CIM, who happened to be at Headquarters, consented saying they could be married after John completed his first year in China.

The week at Headquarters was not long enough for the happy couple. Besides meeting mission personnel and enjoying fellowship with these new co-workers, John had to be outfitted with Chinese clothes. Then it was time to part until the wedding brought them together again in October 1933.

The train that took Betty and the Glittenbergs away from Shanghai was exchanged for a bus through the flat, dusty area of Northern Anhwei Province. John traveled south on a steamship through Southern Anhwei up the Yangtze River. At language school in Anking, he also experienced the frustration of learning Chinese.

Betty learned to use her limited Chinese vocabulary in the city of Fowyang. After settling into the mission compound there, she and her co-worker Katie Dodd, along with a Chinese Bible woman, made an evangelistic trip throughout the region.

Show Illustration #16

The rickshaws creaked and bumped over the rough, rutted mud road jostling the women. Betty looked over the head of her rickshaw man. For as far as she could see the land was flat and dusty. The few buildings nearby were made of mud with thatched roofs. The clusters of trees were choked with the dust from the land. Nearby, a family worked together digging sweet potatoes from mounds of dusty earth.

Show Illustration #17

At mid-afternoon, as the rickshaws bumped along the road, Betty spied a town in the distance. When they got closer, their Chinese woman called, "This is a market town." *What a hubbub,* Betty thought as their rickshaws jerked to a halt.

Men and women, talking, laughing and bargaining loudly, milled around baskets and piles of produce. Betty and Katie handed out tracts as they followed the Bible woman to the inn, a mud house with a courtyard in the back. The people, eager to see two white women, pressed close around them. When they managed to slip into the inn, many people crowded in behind them. With difficulty the landlady shoved the women into a small, dark room off the courtyard for privacy. Again, some of the crowd squeezed in after them. There they watched as the ladies ate. Afterwards, the Bible woman began explaining the Gospel while the girls distributed tracts.

The next day they traveled to a walled city where no missionary had ever lived. A Chinese evangelist and his family occupied the small mission station there. When Betty and her companions arrived, they found the children eager to learn the few Bible choruses the girls knew. The Bible woman preached to group after group of women who packed the chapel for these special meetings. Before leaving, the Chinese women begged Betty and Katie to return and teach them the Bible.

It was a tiring trip, but Betty was encouraged. *Oh, how I long to start Bible classes for the young girls and other meetings for the women and children,* she thought as she bumped back to Fowyang. *What incentive to continue my language study. If only I could communicate more clearly right now!*

Throughout the cold winter months Betty progressed in her language study and was able to communicate more easily with the Chinese. In mid-March, John, down in Anking, passed his first three language exams and even led morning worship in Chinese. In April, John and the other young men in language school were assigned to mission stations throughout the country. John headed to the city of Suancheng to help Mr. and Mrs. Birch instead of taking vacation at the shore during the hot summer months.

The scorching sun turned the summer into the hottest and driest in many years. John was in Suancheng only two months when the Birches left the sweltering city for the cooler hills. They needed the rest, and had to leave John alone with the Chinese Christians.

John accepted this difficult situation good-naturedly. *I should learn a lot of Chinese these next couple of months,* he thought as the Birches left Suancheng in June. *There isn't anyone here who speaks English. I hope the people will be able to understand my poor Chinese and learn something of the Gospel.* Picking up a handful of tracts, he left the mission compound.

Show Illustration #18

Throughout the summer dark-eyed, round-faced children of all ages flocked to the afternoon meetings John held. One way I can teach them is through Scripture choruses, he reasoned. They already know the Chinese tunes. All I need is to teach them the words. In spite of the heat, the children sang lustily, "Yes, Jesus loves me, the Bible tells me so." As they left one day, John thought he understood a child say "parade tomorrow."

Show Illustration #19

The tramp of feet, the banging cymbals, and the wail of voices sounded in the streets the next morning. All day in the shimmering heat the people paraded through the city carrying their idols and praying for rain. The drought continued, and so did parades for several days.

John followed the parade one day, praying for an opportunity to speak to someone about the Lord. As he handed a tract to a young man on the city wall, a crowd gathered. John looked at the people around him. *Help me, Lord,* he prayed, *to make myself understood. Help these people to understand the Gospel.*

Turning to the youth, John asked him to read the tract aloud. The men and women listened intently. John explained the Gospel simply. *I wish I could ask questions,* he thought as he handed out tracts to the others. *But I can understand only a fraction of what they say, and that's not enough to carry on a discussion.* The crowd dispersed, some joining the parade in the distance.

That evening John returned to the city wall. Brilliant crimson rays stretched across the sky behind graying clouds. As the sun sank behind the distant mountains, he bowed his head.

The heavens do declare Your glory, Lord, and the firmament does show Your handiwork, he prayed silently. *How great You are, Lord, and good. Thank You for the joy I have in knowing You. Thank You for the joy I had today explaining the Gospel to the people on this wall. Thank You for the joy I know I shall have in a few weeks when I share these experiences and this view with Betty.*

He raised his head and smiled. "Betty . . . my wife," he whispered. "I like that phrase!"

Chapter 4
Serving Together

Show Illustration #20

The flat-bottomed riverboat moved swiftly with the current, guided by the rowers standing at the square bow. In spite of the pouring rain, the men propelled the vessel with sure strokes. Betty looked out through the cabin door beyond the wet figures at the countryside on either side of the river. The area was known to be bandit territory. *How grateful I am for the rain,* she thought. *It will keep most people–including bandits–indoors.*

A young Chinese student dozed on the seat beside her. Betty glanced at him and tried to stretch her legs without disturbing the boy. *It might have been easier to travel alone,* she thought, *but I couldn't say no when asked to escort him to school. I remember what it's like to travel as a student even though it's been years since I attended school in China.* A scene flashed through her mind as she shifted to a more comfortable position on the hard seat.

How excited my sister Helen and I were back then, Betty mused. *We looked forward to traveling almost around the world with our family. And now, today, I've begun another trip that promises to be just as wonderful. No, it will be even better for this journey is going to make me Mrs. John Stam.* Thinking about that long-awaited day made her smile.

It had been difficult for Betty to leave her fellow workers in Fowyang. She and John would be stationed much farther south and would not see these friends for a long time. But knowing she was leaving to be married made the good-byes easier. And Katie would follow her in several weeks to be one of her bridesmaids.

Show Illustration #13

How much John and I talked of marriage near the end of our days at Moody. Betty closed her eyes, remembering how they chose instead to put God first and go to China separately.

Our last evening together in Chicago was special. Although I was glad to join our friends and pray for China, I was overjoyed at being with John one last time.

It would be several years before we met again, but God knew that was not to be. Seeing John in Shanghai last year was another of the Lord's special surprises. Now in just a few weeks, John will be my husband. It was worth it to put God first and obey Him. He honored our obedience by bringing us together.

Throughout that day and all the next the rain fell on the riverboat as it made its way along. The third day Betty transferred her belongings to a train and finally arrived at her parents' home in Tsinan.

Ten years had passed since Betty had left Tsinan to go to America to attend college. Most of that time she had been away from her parents. Now, throughout September they made plans together for the wedding. And in the middle of October, John arrived from his station.

When morning dawned on October 27, 1933, Betty walked over to the bedroom window and peered out. The sun had risen in the pale blue, cloudless sky. "Thank You, Father, for answering prayer," she said joyfully. "We can have the wedding outdoors after all."

During the morning, carpets were carried from the house to the tennis court. Then long benches were brought from the Chinese church. The wedding party and friends worked together to arrange palms, ferns and bright yellow chrysanthemums at one end of the court. By early afternoon it was transformed into a beautiful outdoor chapel.

Show Illustration #21

By mid-afternoon all guests had arrived. Missionaries and Chinese settled themselves on benches in the improvised chapel. At four o'clock, Marguerite (Betty's roommate from Wilson College and now a missionary in China), Katie and another friend began the processional. Betty followed with her father, her eyes focused on John as she walked slowly down the aisle.

This wedding was different from many Chinese weddings. Instead of keeping her head bowed in fear, Betty looked lovingly into John's face. The ceremony was simple, reverent and joyful, not at all noisy and rowdy. After a reception and dinner with the bridal party, John and Betty left for their honeymoon.

Before the chill of fall changed to the bitter cold of winter, John and Betty arrived at the mission station at Suancheng. The Birches welcomed them. Soon John and Betty had their first home in order. Many evenings they sat at their table, near the warm stove, studying the language. In December they went on their first trip together to one of the outstations in the region. Song the tailor, a faithful Christian who had spent weeks traveling from village to village preaching, went with them.

Show Illustration #22

The village of Swenchiapu, though only about ten miles away, took four hours to reach. Dressed in long Chinese padded (wadded) gowns, John and Betty walked along the narrow road. The small groups of travelers they met stared at them; the more curious asked boldly, "Where do you come from?" John would answer and then ask a question in return.

"Do you read?" he asked an old man resting beside the road.

"No," the man said looking up at John. "But I will take that paper you have in your hand." He reached up for it.

As John opened the brightly colored tract, he thought, *He probably wants this paper for his wife to use when she sews his next pair of shoes. I won't let it be used for soles for his shoes, but I will read it and pray its message will affect his soul.* Then John read the Gospel points and explained them simply.

Show Illustration #23

Arriving in Swenchiapu, John and Betty were welcomed by the Paos. Mr. Pao was a silversmith, a Christian who loved the Lord. Throughout Saturday John and Betty distributed tracts in the town and visited people in their homes. On Sunday, John served his first communion in the morning worship service. That afternoon, Song, Mr. and Mrs. Pao, John and Betty held two open-air meetings. As they began singing, people passing in the street paused, then gathered around. Mr. Pao began preaching.

One woman edged near Betty and fingered her quilted gown. "Nice" she said. Other women surrounded them. Betty smiled and greeted them before Mrs. Pao began teaching. Wide-eyed children peeking from behind their mothers and older children elbowing into the crowd caught Betty's attention. Separating herself from the women, she spoke to the children. They pressed close and listened eagerly to the Bible stories she told.

As the meeting continued, some people drifted away. Their curiosity had been satisfied. Or they were tired of standing. Or they just didn't care to understand this talk about a God who sent His Son to die on a cross as punishment for sin. But other people took their places and Song, Mr. Pao and John preached on and on.

When John and Betty returned to Suancheng (Xuancheng), they continued language study. They talked a lot about going to their own station in the fall. The mission leaders assigned them to Tsingteh (Jingde), a city 60 miles southwest of Suancheng. From there they could visit the surrounding towns and villages in southern Anhwei (Anhui). In February 1934 during the Chinese New Year, John and Betty visited Tsingteh and the area around that mission station.

Show Illustration #24

Two men trotting along the narrow road before them balanced bundles of bedding, clothes, books and food from both ends of the springy poles. Carriers, holding the sedan-chair in which Betty rode, walked with a swinging gait. Stone paths, cut into the mountains, curved and twisted down and up through the valleys. Rice fields climbed the slopes like giant steps. Stone bridges stood over clear-flowing streams. On the horizon, blue peaks of distant ranges edged above the grass-covered mountains.

Every hour the group stopped so the carriers could rest. At large, prosperous inns and small mud huts, John and Betty distributed the colorful Gospel tracts to those who could read. Some purchased Gospels. Everywhere they went there was always an audience. The holiday crowds jostled and shoved each other as they surrounded the tall foreigner and his wife.

"The true and living God of Heaven loves you," John stated. "He has made a way for you, for everyone, to have eternal life." John told the message over and over at each stop and in the inns where they spent their nights.

And then one day the path led into a valley between high mountains. Below lay Tsingteh within a rambling city wall. They made their way down through the trees, past mulberry orchards and tangled vegetation.

A man climbing the path toward them stopped and called, "Welcome to Tsingteh!"

John strode forward and grasped the man's hand. "Thank you for coming to greet us, Mr. Warren," he replied. "It is refreshing to see another CIM missionary in these parts. Betty and I are overjoyed to be here at last."

"Well then, come," Mr. Warren replied. "My wife is expecting you. How are you doing on your first major trip?"

"Quite well, praise God!" John said enthusiastically.

"Good, good," Mr. Warren said. "My wife is eager to show you what will be your home. And I am anxious to introduce you to the people in and around Tsingteh before we leave on furlough."

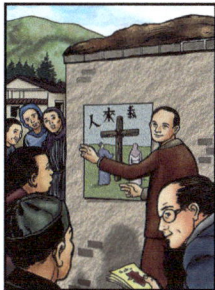

Show Illustration #25

Throughout the week, John and Mr. Warren walked to the villages around the city. In each village square they placed a large Gospel poster on the wall of a building. Passersby gaped at the picture. Some walked closer to investigate and grabbed for the tracts John distributed. When a crowd had gathered, Mr. Warren began preaching.

John watched the men and boys as Mr. Warren explained the Gospel. The Christians joining the missionaries for these open-air meetings listened eagerly, nodding their heads and smiling. Others stared blankly or cocked their heads in a half-interested way. *Oh, Father,* John prayed silently, *help these people understand how to gain eternal life. Encourage the Christians here today. Put a desire in them to tell the Gospel to their friends and neighbors. And help Betty and Mrs. Warren as they teach the women and children.*

The week in Tsingteh passed quickly. John and Betty headed out of the city, walking over a narrow, stone-covered road curving and twisting through the mountains. Twelve miles later, in a valley beneath high mountains, the village of Miaosheo appeared.

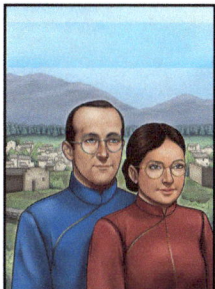

Show Front Cover

"So this is where Mrs. Wang and her son and daughter-in-law live," Betty said to John as they stood side by side looking down at the white-washed buildings scattered below a gently sloping hill bounded by trees.

"Yes," John said, "and this is where Evangelist Lo is coming to live. I am looking forward to working with him."

"The Wangs will be glad to have their own pastor," Betty added. "I wonder if others in Miaosheo will believe as quickly as Mrs. Wang did. Isn't it wonderful that she believed the first time she heard the Gospel many years ago? She must be quite old now. Her husband is dead, isn't he?"

"Yes," John said. "Let's find where she lives. Perhaps we can arrange a meeting with the Christians for tomorrow morning, the Lord's Day."

Mrs. Wang welcomed Betty and John, a smile lighting her wrinkled face. Stepping carefully on tiny bound feet, she led them into the great, old mansion that was her home. She hovered over them as they rested, preparing food she knew they would enjoy.

What a dear, godly woman she is, Betty thought.

The next morning the Christians living in the country arrived by ones and twos. Sitting off to one side, Betty watched as they listened to John preach. *How eager they are to hear the Word of God,* she thought. *If only we could stay and not have to return to Suancheng. I long to teach the women and children about You, Father. Please use John and me in such a way that these Christians and others in Miaosheo will learn to know You and have the peace that only You can give in these troubled times.*

Back on the path the next day, they left Miaosheo behind a bend in the trail. Trekking over high mountain passes and down into valleys, they visited other villages and groups of Christians. Then they returned to Suancheng.

The frustration of never knowing enough Chinese words to communicate clearly prompted John and Betty to study harder. Word by word they increased their vocabulary, making these new words part of their conversations with the Chinese.

John went out often to distribute tracts and witness. Betty remained close to the mission compound preparing for the baby she would have in the fall. As summer began, they went to Wuhu, a city along the Yangtze River. John took the place of the local mission secretary who was away on vacation.

Show Illustration #26

On September 11, 1934, Helen Priscilla was born in the Methodist Hospital.

"Don't you think she looks like you, John?" Betty asked as her husband held the tiny baby. "She has your mouth and chin."

"And a lot of black hair," John interrupted. "She's the cutest little thing, but not when she cries," he continued, handing the whimpering infant back to Betty. "I'm glad your mother is coming to help you care for Helen. I feel better about leaving to check on things in Tsingteh knowing you'll be well cared for."

"I'll be fine, John," Betty said. "I know you're anxious to return to our station. Don't you like the sound of that? Our station. Please greet Mrs. Wang for me. I'm eager to see her again."

John left Betty at Wuhu and traveled down into Southern Anhwei. Erwin Kohfield, another CIM missionary, went with him. Together they visited village after village, distributing tracts and famine relief money. The drought that summer had ruined most of the harvest in the area.

In Miaosheo John and Erwin handed out tracts in the street and spoke to the Chinese about the way of salvation. Then they went to Mrs. Wang's home. After a meal, John waited for some of the Christians to arrive. The evening had cooled and the house was damp. Just before he began the Bible study, Mrs. Wang's daughter-in-law ran from the room. John was perplexed until he saw her return and place a shawl around Mrs. Wang's shoulders. *How considerate,* he thought. *Truly, Christ is present in these Chinese believers. Their love for You is shown in how they care for each other in even the little needs of life.*

Show Illustration #27

Opening his Bible, John read aloud Psalm 22, 23 and 24. The room was still as he told about the suffering Saviour, the good Shepherd and the King of Glory. "One day the Lord Jesus Christ will return," he concluded. "What a wonderful day that will be!"

Leaving Miaosheo the next day, John and Erwin walked to Tsingteh. *Soon this will be home,* John thought as they walked through the gate in the city wall. *But only if there are no Communists in the area. It would never be safe to bring Betty and the baby here if they are around.*

That day the Tsingteh District Magistrate assured them, "No, no! No Communists around. Bandits, yes–sometimes, but district is quiet with no Communist activity now. Come with wife and child. If there is danger, come to my yamen and you will be safe."

John returned to Wuhu with a lighter heart. "There doesn't seem to be any reason why we shouldn't move to Tsingteh," he said to Erwin. "While the government troops are pushing the Communists out of the province below us into our area, things seem quiet there. But we must pray that the mission leaders make the right decision about when we should move down. Our heavenly Father knows what we should do."

Chapter 5

Triumph over Death

Show Illustration #26

John walked into the room where Betty was finishing dressing Helen. He picked up the baby. "It's been decided, Betty," he said joyfully. "We can leave for Tsingteh as soon as we are ready."

"Oh, John," Betty cried excitedly. "That won't take long. We have our cook, and the other little woman will be a fine helper for me even though she is blind in one eye. We just need to go back to Suancheng to pack our belongings. I'm eager to show the baby to the Birches."

"Do you think we could leave by November 12?" John asked.

"I'm sure of it," Betty replied.

The short-term Bible school was in session when John and Betty arrived in Suancheng. John proudly carried Helen to the chapel. There he showed her to the key Christians from the country villages who had been studying Scriptures together for several weeks. The next Sunday in a Chinese service, John and Betty dedicated Helen to the Lord. (Dedication is a special service when parents present their children to the Lord and determine to raise them to serve Him.) The next day they set out for Tsingteh.

Show Illustration #24

As their belongings were bumped along on wheelbarrows ahead of them, Betty and the baby rode a sedan-chair over the mountain roads. John walked nearby. As before, they stopped at each village to hand out tracts and speak to the Chinese. Starting, stopping and talking stretched the 60 mile journey into several days. On November 23 they walked into *their* valley. Tsingteh lay below them.

"Our station, John," Betty said as she stepped from the sedan-chair and looked down over the trees at the walled city.

"And in it are souls who need to hear the Gospel," John said seriously. "I pray we will take every opportunity and be bold in our witness for God."

Descending, they passed through one of the city gates and headed for the house the Warrens had secured for them before going on furlough. It was a large, old, Chinese house. John quickly set up a couple of stoves to keep at least one room warm. Betty arranged their few belongings. Above their desk she hung a plaque with the words "Jesus Never Fails."

Whatever happens in our ministry here in Tsingteh, Jesus will never fail us. What a wonderful promise, she thought, then turned the words into a prayer. *Help us to remember this, Father, when the work becomes difficult or we are in danger. Our times are in Your hands.*

John stuck his head through the door. "If everything is fairly settled here, Betty, I'm going to make our presence known to the Magistrate. And I want to put up some posters in the street chapel out front."

"We can use the chapel then for our first Sunday service," Betty remarked.

"I'll begin inviting people on my way to and from the Magistrate," John said, heading out to the stone-flagged street.

Show Illustration #28

The first Sunday only two strangers attended the service. But during the week the chapel was open three times. Little groups pressed into the room. The women, touching the baby Betty held, would exclaim noisily to each other about what she wore. Betty spoke kindly to the women, always trying to talk about the Lord.

John spoke directly to the men, reading from his Chinese Bible and pointing to the Gospel posters to illustrate his words. The men were attentive, but slow to respond. As the group straggled out of the chapel one afternoon, John prayed silently, *Help these people, Father. Open their minds to understand the Gospel. Bring some to the place where they will come to You for salvation.*

That night John turned from the desk where he had been writing. "I've just written the mission headquarters that I plan to go to Miaosheo this weekend with Pastor Chen to meet Evangelist Lo. I've already written Lo saying we would join him this Friday, December 7, for evangelistic meetings. He should be moved into the Gospel Hall in Miaosheo by then."

Betty looked up from the chair where she was folding some baby clothes. "Do you think it is safe to travel that far, John? Have you heard any new reports of Communists in the area?"

"There was one report today, Betty. But you know how all the other reports have been false since we've been here. We won't leave until Friday. I want to preach in the street chapel several more times this week before going. We must take every opportunity to tell these people the Gospel."

Show Illustration #29

Several days later on Thursday morning, Betty was bathing Helen when she heard a commotion in the street. In a few minutes John entered the room.

"That was the second messenger from the Magistrate," he said slowly. "It seems in the last hour or so since the first messenger brought a warning, they've heard that a large Communist unit is approaching Tsingteh. This messenger says several thousand soldiers are only four miles from the city."

"What should we do, John?" Betty asked as she dried the baby.

"Well, I think I'll go check these reports," he replied. "Maybe they are only rumors. But just in case, we should prepare to leave." He turned to the servants and asked them to hire carriers and get sedan-chairs ready. Then he left.

Betty dressed Helen. Crossing the room, she removed ten dollars from the small amount of cash, then returned to the baby. Carefully she bundled the infant in a zippered suit. But before pulling up the zipper, she tucked some diapers around the baby and pinned the money to them. "Just in case," she whispered as she lifted Helen and held her close.

After a while John returned. "All the reports are conflicting, Betty," he said. "But let's get ready to leave."

Before they had gathered much together, rifle shots sounded in the distance. Betty looked quickly to John. "Lock the gates," he said to the cook. "Then come back. We must pray to our Father." When the cook returned, the four knelt to pray.

The shots soon resounded in the street along with loud yelling and tramping of feet. Then a wild banging thundered through their premises. And in a few minutes they listened to fists pounding on their door. John crossed the room and opened it, inviting the soldiers in.

Several soldiers pushed through the doorway and looked around. The red stars on their uniforms and three red stripes on their coat collars identified them as Communists. One stepped forward and addressed John rudely, "Give us your money."

While John emptied their purses, Betty offered the soldiers tea, but they rejected it. Suddenly they grabbed John, bound his hands, and shoved him out of the house. They soon returned and took Betty and the baby to the prison where John was held. Later John was escorted back to their home to find food for Helen.

"There is nothing left!" the little one-eyed woman cried. "The Communists have seized everything." She broke down and sobbed.

"Never mind, Mrs. Mei. Don't be afraid," John said consolingly. "Our heavenly Father knows what we need. Now you go sleep with old Mrs. Li tonight." Then he was marched back to the prison.

As looting continued in the city, John pondered what he should write to the mission headquarters. Finally he penciled this:

At four o'clock the next morning, the Communists roused John and Betty and hustled them onto the stone road to Miaosheo. Betty rode a horse part of the way over the winding trail while John walked with Helen.

Show Illustration #30

In Miaosheo they were thrust into the post office under guard. The thousands of soldiers who had hurried the missionary captives along now rushed through the city and ransacked it. As Betty sat down and took the baby from John, the postmaster asked, "Where are they taking you? Where are you going?"

"I don't know where they are going," John replied steadily. "But I know this, we *ARE* going to Heaven."

The postmaster looked at them in bewilderment. Then, understanding what John said, and touched by what it meant, he left them alone for a moment. Returning, he walked over to Betty. "Here, take this fruit. You must eat. And you, too," he said offering some to John.

"No," John replied. "I wish to write a letter, but I have no money to send it. Will you please forward it anyway?"

"Yes, yes," the postmaster nodded. "When the mail goes out, your letter will go."

John took the paper and wrote a second letter to the mission. He handed it to the postmaster, then joined Betty and waited.

China Inland Mission, Shanghai

Tsingteh, An
Dec. 6, 1934

Dear Brethren,

My wife, baby and myself are today in the hands of the Communists, in the city of Tsingteh. Their demand is $20,000 for our release.

All our possessions and stores are in their hands, but we praise God for peace in our hearts and a meal tonight. God grant you wisdom in what you do, and us fortitude, courage and peace of heart. He is able–and a wonderful Friend in such a time. Things happened so quickly this a.m. They were in the city just a few hours after the ever persistent rumors really became alarming, so that we could not prepare to leave in time. We were just too late.

The Lord bless and guide you, and as for us, may God be glorified whether by life or by death.

In Him,
John C. Stam

The sky was darkening when soldiers came and took John and Betty and the baby through the village to an abandoned house. Once owned by a rich man, the place was deserted. In a room off the inner courtyard, they tied John to a bed post. Betty was free to care for Helen. Again they waited through the long night, guards outside their door.

Saturday morning their captors demanded they remove their outer quilted garments. Tying their hands behind their backs, the soldiers pushed John and Betty out into the street. Other Communists were shouting to the people, "Come see the foreign devils die."

Show Illustration #31

Through the chaos, John and Betty walked calmly among the terror-stricken Chinese. Out through the city gate and up Eagle Hill they were paraded. When the proclamation "The foreign devils must die!" was shouted again, one man broke from the crowd and fell on his knees. John recognized him. Chang was one of the Christians, a medicine seller.

"Do not kill these people," Chang pleaded.

"Quiet!" a soldier roared.

"No, no. Release these good people," he cried again.

Several soldiers leaped at Chang and dragged him to his feet. "We'll take care of you later," one hissed. (Chang was killed later.)

As John turned to speak to the leader of the band, a voice cried, "Kneel!" Barely had he fallen on one knee when a flash of a sword struck his throat and ended his life. Betty trembled a little, but then the same sword struck her neck from behind and she joined John in Heaven.

The Communist soldiers dashed into the woods outside the city when they heard shooting in the distance. The Chinese of Miaosheo scurried back to what was left of their homes. The bodies of John and Betty were left on the hill all that day as government troops fired on the Communists.

Show Illustration #32

High in the hills where they had fled, Evangelist Lo, the Wangs and others watched the skirmish between the two armies. Another refugee joined them. "The Communists have captured a foreigner," he told the little group. "I don't know who it is."

"Perhaps it's the Roman Catholic priest from Tsingteh," Evangelist Lo commented. "I hope the Stams escaped before the Communists arrived."

The battle continued throughout the afternoon. More villagers fled into the hills. One refugee told Lo, "A foreigner and his wife were killed this morning." The Christians were horrified. "The Stams," Lo whispered.

Darkness fell across the valley. The Wangs and Lo family huddled together on the hillside. Suddenly a burst of light lit the valley. Flames leaped up around a house in the village. A while later, a second fire farther away burned another home. "The Communists are setting fires to the houses as they retreat," Lo said sorrowfully. "Will there be anything left when they leave?"

Sunday morning Evangelist Lo and the Wangs crept from the hillside down into the village. There Lo learned how the Stams were martyred. "But the baby," he said, "where is she?" Those he asked lowered their eyes and turned away, afraid to help him. Communists might still be around and hear them. It was safer to ignore Lo's pleas. Finally one lady nodded toward a house. As Lo entered the deserted building, he heard a baby crying. Quickly he raced through the courtyards. In the bedroom off the inner courtyard all alone, Helen Priscilla lay crying on the bed. Lo picked her up and headed for the Wangs' home.

But there was still something else Lo wanted to do. Slowly he walked out of Miaosheo and up Eagle Hill. There he found the bodies of John and Betty. Returning to town, he and the Wangs obtained coffins. A crowd gathered as Evangelist Lo, Mrs. Wang and her son lovingly placed the bodies in the coffins. After praying, Lo turned to the crowd.

"These people," he said pointing to the wooden boxes, "are children of God. They are now in God's presence for their spirits are unharmed. They came to China, to Miaosheo, to tell you about God and His love so that you might believe in Him and be saved. You have heard the message they preached. Repent and believe." As Lo spoke, the Chinese began to weep.

After placing the coffins in a safe place in town, Evangelist Lo turned to his wife, "We must hire a carrier and take the baby to Wuhu."

Show Illustration #33

Early in the morning several days later, Mrs. Lo gently placed Helen in one rice basket while her husband tucked their son into the other basket. A carrier balanced his long pole over his shoulder, stood, and followed the Los out of Miaosheo.

All of their possessions had been looted by the Communists, but Mrs. Lo had found the ten dollars tucked in Helen's zippered suit. That was enough for their trip.

In villages along the way, Chinese women nursed Helen. In one town they found a tin of powdered milk which Mrs. Lo knew how to prepare. She even had a bottle. The 100-mile trek through the mountains continued for several days. But no bandits stopped them and they saw no Communists.

On December 14 the Los arrived at the mission home in Suancheng, then headed for the hospital in Wuhu where missionaries met them. Helen was safe. Later, her grandparents (Betty's parents) took her to live with them in Tsinan.

The news of John and Betty's martyrdom flashed around the world in newspapers and magazine articles. As their story was told and read, many young people offered to go overseas as missionaries. Moody Bible Institute held a memorial service for the Stams in January 1935. At the end of a day of prayer, seven hundred students stood to indicate they would go wherever God would lead them. Nearby, in Wheaton College, another 200 students made the same commitment. Many of these young men and women went to the mission field, some to China.

Today, God is still looking for people to go wherever He leads. It may be here in your country or it may be overseas. But, wherever it is, God wants people to be prepared to serve Him.

- Is Jesus your Saviour? When John and Betty were young, they asked the Lord Jesus to forgive their sin and become their Saviour.
- Have you surrendered your life to Him? Betty did. At a Keswick Bible Conference she determined to live each day to please God.
- Do you trust God to supply your needs? John learned to trust God. He discovered God would give him what he *needed*.
- Are you learning how to serve Him now by witnessing to your friends? Betty and John began witnessing to people in America before they went to China.
- Will you say to God, "Here is my life. I, too, want to go wherever You lead me. I want to serve You as John and Betty did."

Teacher: Conclude with appropriate invitation and prayer. Provide necessary counseling. Follow up decisions with encouraging notes, phone calls or visits. Stimulate interest in missions.

Helen Stam grew up happily with her cousins. Following her mother's and aunts' example, she graduated from Wilson College, and later from the Presbyterian School of Christian Education in Richmond, VA. She spent a number of years as a Christian educator in various positions. She then worked as an editorial writer for a firm in a large Eastern city until her retirement.

Epilogue

News of the martyrdom of John and Betty Stam shocked the Western church. The first reaction was, "What a tragedy!" Then people began asking, "Can I go and fill their place?" Hundreds of young people volunteered for mission service throughout the world as the result of the death of that one young couple.

In China, the Stam's martyrdom was followed by more kidnappings, torture and destruction by the Chinese Communists on their Long March from Southeast to Northwest China. Pastors and missionaries alike knew that they must prepare the church for a possible Communist takeover.

China's government and way of life were disrupted in the 1930s. Japan saw this and decided to invade the country. In July 1937 the Japanese Imperial Army came down out of Manchuria into Peking, beginning the eight-year-long Sino-Japanese War. The bombing of Pearl Harbor by the Japanese on December 7, 1941, dragged America into the conflict and made China one of the battlefields of World War II.

With Japan attacking China from the outside and with the Communists, like termites, destroying the country from the inside, the China Inland Mission took steps to strengthen the church and prepare it for an uncertain future:

- Local churches were organized into associations.
- Missionaries and church leaders opened lay training institutes.
- Older Bible schools were expanded and new ones opened.
- Student ministries were started in many of the large state-operated universities.

As the Japanese War continued, missionaries of all denominations chose to stay on with the churches. After Pearl Harbor hundreds of missionaries and their children were confined in concentration camps in China by the Japanese. Other missionaries fled west with refugees by boat, cart or on foot. Sixty million people relocated in Western China to escape the endless bombing of Chinese cities by Japanese warplanes.

During all the turmoil, terror and tragedy from the 1930s to 1949, the churches grew steadily. Most remarkable was the growth of the indigenous Chinese groups that had no organizational links with Western missions–the True Jesus Church, the Jesus family and the Assembly Hall, or "Little Flock," as many called them. At the same time, God raised up gifted pastors and evangelists such as Wang Ming-Tao, David Yang, John Sung, Andrew Gih and Watchman Nee. They were God's lighthouses of faith to illumine the darkness ahead.

When the Japanese surrendered on V-J Day in 1945, fewer than 1,000 missionaries were left in China. The long, grinding years of war had taken their toll. By 1948, however, the total had climbed back to over 3,000. In 1949 baptized believers totaled just over three quarters of a million.

All during the years of the Japanese War, Mao Zedung and his Communist armies were biding their time in rural North China. Encouraged and supplied by the Russians, they burst into the cities, then spread south and west. By 1949 enough of China was in their hands for Mao Zedung to declare on October 1 of that year the founding of the People's Republic of China. Chiang Kai-shek and his Nationalist army had been defeated more by corruption and dissension than by actual fighting on the battlefield. They fled to Taiwan.

What happened to the missionaries during these earth-shaking events? The Communist authorities pressured Chinese churches to convince the missionaries that they must leave so it would not look as if the Communists were throwing out the missionaries. But out they wanted them, in no uncertain terms. Premier Zhou Enlai told a company of church leaders whom he summoned to Beijing. "When you clean house you don't want any guests around." The churchmen passed the word down the line.

And "clean house" the Communists did. Between 1949 and 1955 they killed 35 million of their own best people–teachers, doctors, lawyers, bankers, merchants, industrialists, land owners–anyone who might possibly oppose them in the future.

The Communist party and government established a department to deal with religion. The branch of this department which was to oversee all Protestants was called the Three-Self Patriotic Movement (TSPM). Communism was seeking to control the church from within. Pastors and other church leaders were arrested and tried; thousands of them died. Thousands of others suffered in prison year after terrible year.

The church survived the initial attacks, but halfway through the violent Cultural Revolution the church seemed to disappear. Church buildings became factories, Bible schools and seminaries were closed, public meetings were stopped and Bibles were destroyed. The church became invisible to many.

It was then that the house church movement began. These cell-like groups, informal and (strictly speaking) illegal, grew during the Cultural Revolution and have grown by leaps and bounds since 1978. Though the TSPM was made the official church after Mao Zedung's death in 1976, by far the majority of Chinese believers (some say 95%) are connected with the house churches, not the officially approved TSPM.

The Chinese church has certainly grown. From less than 1,000,000 baptized believers in 1949, Christians today may number as many as 50 million. In 1949, one Chinese in 600 was a believer; today there may be as many as one in 20. In spite of terror, trials and torture, the Chinese Church has not only survived, it has increased.

What do you think are the reasons for this?

- the Bible in the language of the people.
- Christian broadcasts from outside China.
- the steadfastness under stress of multitudes of Chinese believers.
- the faithfulness, even unto death, of those who have gone before, such as John and Betty Stam.

Chapter 1

1. Who was the little girl who went to China as a baby with her parents? *(Betty Scott)*
2. Why did her parents go to China? *(They were missionaries.)*
3. Why was Betty so sure that she was going to Heaven? *(She believed that Jesus had died for her sins and rose again. She had asked Him to forgive her wrong doings.*
4. What kind of schooling did Betty have? *(She studied at home until she was 11, then attended a boarding school near Beijing.)*
5. What was so exciting about the trip Betty and her family took when she was 16? *(They traveled around the world for six months seeing lots of interesting, famous places.)*
6. Who was one of the first friends Betty met at college? Why was she so special? *(Marguerite; she was a freshman like Betty; she visited Betty when she was in the infirmary.)*
7. When Betty attended a Bible conference in New Jersey, what did she discover about herself? *(She learned that God wanted her to live for Him, not for herself.)*
8. Can you remember the Bible verse that changed Betty's life? *("To me to live is Christ, and to die is gain.")*
9. Where did Betty go after she graduated from college and why? What did she do there? *(She went to Moody Bible Institute because she wanted to lead people to Christ. She visited prisons and took part in street meetings.)*
10. By now Betty knew God was calling her to be a missionary to China. Why did she go to the Page home on Monday evenings and whom did she meet there? *(She and other young people prayed for mission work in China. She met John Stam who also was interested in going to China.)*

Chapter 2

1. What was the custom in the Stam home before the evening meal? *(They would read together from the Bible.)*
2. John came from a family of eight children. What were a lot of them involved in? *(They helped at the Star of Hope Mission, taking part in open-air meetings and visitation.)*
3. What did John want to do with his life after grammar school? *(He attended business school and dreamed of working and earning money.)*
4. How did John feel about the work of missionaries? *(He did not want to take part in the work very much, feeling that he knew about God and that was enough.)*
5. What happened one night at a meeting of the mission when John was 15? *(John realized the awful state that he was in—ignoring God and trying to live without Him. He confessed his sin and decided to follow God.)*
6. After John graduated from business school, he worked several years in New Jersey and New York City. What decision did he make and why? *(He decided to return to school to study the Bible and learn how to teach or preach. Helping people find God was more important than making money.)*
7. What school did John go to and how would he pay his way? *(He went to Moody Bible Institute in Chicago. When his money ran out, he would trust God to provide the rest.)*
8. What did John learn at Moody about the people of China? *(He learned that there were many thousands in inland China who had never heard of the Lord Jesus.)*
9. How did John feel about going to China as a missionary? *(He was very interested–the need was great and there was no good reason for him to stay home.)*
10. Who was John interested in at the Monday meetings of the China Inland Mission? What was his prayer about her? *(Betty Scott; John asked God to help him to trust Him to make it possible so they could get to know each other.)*

Chapter 3

1. What did Betty learn in college about God's provision for her needs? *(She realized she had been complaining about God's care for her needs. She needed to learn to trust Him.)*
2. What truth did John and Betty face concerning their future? *(They had to put God first and obey Him. If He wanted them to be married, He would bring them together in China.)*
3. Who went to China first? What did the other one do? *(Betty went first while John finished his schooling at Moody.)*
4. What was it like to be a missionary in China in the early 1930's? *(It was difficult and dangerous. Missionaries risked their lives to tell the Chinese of Christ.)*
5. What was the first thing Betty had to do on reaching China? *(She went to language school with 60 other young women. Learning to speak and write it was difficult.)*
6. When John went to China, what blessing did God give John and Betty? *(Betty "just happened" to be in Shanghai when John's ship arrived there. While together, they made plans to be married after John's first year in China.)*
7. What did Betty do on the evangelistic trip she made with her co-worker and the Chinese Bible woman? *(She and Katie handed out Gospel tracts to the Chinese people they met.)*
8. How did the trip encourage Betty? *(She was motivated to keep studying Chinese so she could communicate with the women and children in their language.)*
9. What problems did John face in his first year? *(Being able to communicate the Gospel was very hard as he still did not have a good enough knowledge of the language.)*
10. Why do you think that it was a good idea for John and Betty to be apart for a year? *(They needed to learn the language and get out among the people and interact with them. They could concentrate on this better while apart.)*

Chapter 4

1. Can you name some of the methods of transportation John and Betty used in China? *(Rickshaw, train, bus, steamship, riverboat, sedan-chair, walking)*
2. Fill in the missing words in this testimony Betty gave before her wedding: "Now in just a few weeks, John will be my _____. It was worth it to put ____ first and obey Him. He honored our _____ by bringing us together." *(Husband, God, obedience)*
3. What words would you use to describe their wedding? *(Outdoors, simple, reverent, joyful, beautiful, happy)*
4. What were some of the ways the Stams as well as the Chinese Christians ministered with the Chinese people? *(They visited villages, gave out tracts, sang songs, told Bible stories, preached in open-air meetings, put up Gospel posters.)*
5. Why was it important to make these trips to mission stations and the area around them? *(They needed to go where the people were, to meet them and talk to them instead of waiting for the people to come to them.)*
6. What happened in John and Betty's life on September 11, 1934? *(Their daughter Helen Priscilla was born.)*
7. Who were some of the Chinese Christians John and Betty knew? *(Song, the tailor; Mr. and Mrs. Pao; Mrs. Wang and her son and daughter-in-law; Evangelist Lo)*
8. Who were greatly feared in China at this time in history and why? *(The Communists and bandits; they would rob people and sometimes kill them, even missionaries.)*

9. What kind of clothes did John and Betty wear? *(Quilted gowns like the Chinese people wore)*

Chapter 5

1. What special occasion happened for Helen Priscilla at a Chinese church service? *(She was dedicated to the Lord.)*
2. On their way to Tsingteh, what did John and Betty do at each village? *(They handed out tracts and talked to the people.)*
3. Do you remember the words on the plaque that Betty put up over their desk? What were they? *("Jesus Never Fails")*
4. Who came to Tsingteh not long after the Stams got there? *(The Communist soldiers)*
5. Where were the Stams taken by the soldiers? *(To prison)*
6. What else did the soldiers do? *(They looted the city, taking things that did not belong to them, including John and Betty's belongings.)*
7. The postmaster in Miaosheo asked the Stams where the soldiers were taking them. What did John reply? *(He said that he didn't know where the soldiers were going but that they were going to Heaven.)*
8. At John and Betty's funeral, what did the people of the village get to hear one more time? *(They heard an invitation by Evangelist Lo to repent and believe.)*
9. Where was baby Helen found and what was pinned to her clothes? *(She was found on the bed in the house where the soldiers had taken her parents before they were killed. The $10 that her mother had put there was what was pinned to her clothes.)*
10. What was the response to John and Betty's death by students at Moody Bible Institute and Wheaton College? *(Almost 700 young people dedicated their lives to follow wherever God would lead them.)*